ABSENT PEOPLE, ABSENT PLACES

SARANYA SUBRAMANIAN is a poet, writer, and founder of The Bombay Poetry Crawl. An MFA in Writing graduate from the University of San Francisco, her writing has been published in *Frontline*, *Lithub*, *The Bombay Literary Magazine*, *The Caravan*, *Madras Courier*, *South Asian Avant Garde*, *Outlook*, *Vayavya*, *Kitaab*, *Museum of Art & Photography*, *Scroll.in* and *Yearbook of Indian Poetry*, and her poems have been nominated for the Best of the Net 2024 awards.

Saranya's essay 'The Cockroach and I' was published by Penguin Random House after winning runner-up to the Financial Times/Bodley Head Essay Prize in 2020. She has performed poetry for TEDx, at G5A, held workshops and literary sessions for the Emily Dickinson Museum, Jehangir Nicholson Art Foundation, Project 88, Carleton College, Kala Ghoda Arts Festival, as well as other art and education institutions. And she writes because, well, that's all she can really do.

ABSENT PEOPLE, ABSENT PLACES

SARANYA SUBRAMANIAN

WESTLAND
POETRY

WESTLAND
POETRY

Published by Westland Books, a division of Nasadiya Technologies Private Limited, in 2026

No. 269/2B, First Floor, 'Irai Arul', Vimalraj Street, Nethaji Nagar, Alapakkam Main Road, Maduravoyal, Chennai 600095

Westland and the Westland logo are the trademarks of Nasadiya Technologies Private Limited, or its affiliates.

ISBN: 9789371970549

10 9 8 7 6 5 4 3 2 1

Typeset by Jojy Philip

Printed at Manipal Technologies Limited, Manipal

for amma and appa and akka

Dear Reader,

I wrote *Absent People, Absent Places* as a collection of poems that observe the trajectory of depression in its colourful, varied, multiplicitous forms: from absence, fighting absence, finding presence, to presence. For the speaker of these poems, recovery and growth from depression leads to the ultimate telos of self-acceptance. The poems mark the simultaneous devolvement of the speaker and the nation she is part of, and witness her coming to terms with flaws—her own, and the nation state's. If absence is the complete rejection of the self, then presence lies in unabashed acceptance. If absence represents the disintegration of the nation, then presence represents recognising and piecing together the fragments, however fractured. Through the non-linear, looping journey towards acceptance, the speaker asserts herself: this is who I am; this is where we are. This is who we've become. Accepting one's own complicity in an unequal social order is as important as accepting personal shortcomings. This acknowledgement is what helps us remain in the present.

Being in the present is one of the biggest challenges in the new age, but it is also the most powerful weapon against absence. And this presence must be celebrated.

Contents

ஒன்று: Absence

இரண்டு: Fighting Absence, Finding Presence

மூன்று: Presence

ஒன்று
Absence

That speeding train—
it *is* my life.
Those *are* my hands—
split ends of sabotage.

– from 'Missing Person' by Adil Jussawalla

At Night, By Myself

i kick cats,
doom scroll thru the blue,
picture marrying you

stack up my days
like used styrofoam plates
one atop the other

say all the words
we're not supposed to say
(yes, even *that* one)

imagine my best friend dying
and all the beautiful things i'd say
at her funeral

who i really am
leaks out
wouldn't you love me now

Travelling

everywhere i am
it is all new
and new-smelling with trees
with ripe foreign fruits
with englishness
in fast cars and bullet trains—
everywhere i am
it is all new and i am
here, in the present
loving every minute

i am stranded
here, it is exhausting
moving and growing
cutting my trilingual tongue
to keep up, ending up
in compartments of isolation;
i am stranded:
an absent person
discarding my old life
until the novelty wears off

Unpacking Academia

This hefty bag of classroom conversations,
this calm of guilt that comes with frequent
acquittals.

One bright white light blinks
through the tissue paper night. This city
is made up of towel roads that soak up
the sea and fish and blood and saline.

Did you know melancholia is a jittery
feeling that paints billboards post midnight
so we have something to talk about

during car rides. An auto rickshaw wallah
and his wife were busted by the cops for selling
their fifth baby for ninety thousand (not one lakh).
Impressive; strategy like a marketing agency's.

May the walls of our classes be forever lit up, may
our corridors hunch like gallows, may we live
in our own prisons, glued to luxury, reckoning

with our lives in the sanctity of textbooks and theory—

Overheard in Modi's India, 2021
A Golden Shovel After Ilya Kaminsky

'If you ask me, India has a PR problem. It's not like we
are *all* bad, or poor, or dying. They should focus on the lived
lives, the lives we're living. Last weekend we happily

drove to the farm and the cops were so nice—that, too, during
this awful time. See, I like to focus on the good. Unlike the
media that focuses on our flaws and deaths and wars.'

Stillnesses

City lights crescendo into a single line—
an accidental shot, a momentary breath,
blood spurts out of a body—

an accidental shot, a momentary breath,
a still body held upright by an airplane belt, tightening
organs, shooting through the sky—

an accidental shot, a momentary breath
released during turbulence. What turbulent
times we live in, what terrific

violences circle one another: which
do you think will kill us faster?
A nation apologising, a leader leading

a campaign of apologies: Apologise
or Go Back to Pakistan, *Go Back*
-wards in time to the last time

you saw a grey hair stretching
out of your scalp and watch it water
down your back. Meanwhile,
tragedies encircle this ancient rock, this ancient
heart fighting stillness, this brand
new soul searching for a history;

heritage is, after all, a choice. A sweating
body, a breathless body lusting after language, full
-stopping after every
word, desperate for time to stop,
for this blanket to harden into armour,
for night to fall heavily on me, to concretise

this moment. Feet wanting both lethargy
and movement, elbows pushing time
outward: keep place for me here, please

remember me, please
hold me please
please, please stop

right here. An accidental shot,
a momentary breath; the very millisecond
before disaster.

Night Windows
After Edward Hopper

These days, nights slime over the window
frame and slink into my home. I'm somewhere
between Jivakoti and Isvarakoti, somewhere
between texting a new boy and wanting to die.
If I am to first negate the world before affirming
it, if I am to want ultimate freedom, how do I
gently tell this to my body, how do I gently let
my body down? Everything is funny to Wallace
at Walgreens, but at least he tells me jokes when
I'm there at midnight hunting for melatonin.
He asks me what's up, I debate whether or not
I should tell him that everything hurts: my top
right molar and my heart, but both dental care
and therapy are exorbitant in your country. Instead
I say, eh, not much, just can't sleep. He nods and
smiles, tells me a joke, I walk back home, hoping
that the guy from the bus stop doesn't follow me
once again. Can't tell the time at home anymore;
three clocks on my phone anxiously tick between
three continents, the oven clock's been off since
before I moved in, and I don't think anyone's awake
in any of the places I know. Should check what time
it is, should check when the grocery store opens
so I can buy milk and bread and other things
to sustain this life so I can keep on living, should

probably shower today, should wash the dishes
or unpack or clean my room, should probably pop
a Crocin to flatten the fever that's rising in my skin.
It's burning; the sun must be close; it should rise soon.

Ghazal for the Absent Person – I

During the year of death, I became an absent person.
A bodiless body of yearning: that is an absent person.

Existing in slices during the day's ripest hours,
shapeshifting is what shapes the absent person.

I've mastered how to edge through sunrays, shed
all sense of presence, become an absent person,

learning it's best to petal at night. Best to fold out
as a paper sky, best to unspool into an absent person.

To represent all emptiness, all things void, to
defend meaninglessness is to be an absent person.

You can find me at thresholds, borders, bordering
black holes; event horizons populated by absent persons.

Named to protect all futilities, gatekeeper
of worthless words: it is I, the absent person.

Ghazal for the Absent Person – II

Living life in anticipation of you, முருகா, is to be an absent person.
To collapse all time by singing to you is to be an absent person.

Most of this lifetime is spent waiting to be fucked,
erased, eroded—to be turned into an absent person.

To be kept by another body, to be pocketed in tenderness,
to forget one's own self is to become an absent person.

The reason is simple: என்ன கவி பாடினாலும் உந்தன் மனம்
இரங்கவில்லை. You have turned humans into absent persons.

You, with your peacock beauty, இன்னும் என்ன
சோதனையா? How cruel to create absent persons

tied to the world, how cruel to give us the song of முருகா
to sing, only to be muted out, sidelined as absent persons.

I shudder at the thought of another lifetime: another century spent
away from you, away from home, in the present, not absent. Person

-hood is doomed to live circularly in violence. Saranya, the Sufis say, दिल्ली
अभी दूर है, but one day I'll be with you, and we will both be absent persons.

Synonyms For...

a skyless city: fog marches in, acts/
as a roof/ unkempt homes: give way for spiders
to crawl through/ open hearts: aired out
by south-west monsoons/ opened bodies: surrendered
to surgical tools/ morning meditations: pierce
walls, calming every room/ morning vibrations: settle
into quietude/ charged up neurons: burn
with rage, shoot up to the brain/ daily: an orange yolk
sizzles on a blue saucepan of sky, scrambling light/ and later,
when things cool down, i'm still not me: there's been
an insurgence into the bloodstream/ pity: naive mind
so easily seduced/ naive child believes exactly what she wants to.

Stupid Lover

'What thereby closes off the lover's language is the very thing which has instituted it: fascination.'
–Roland Barthes, *A Lover's Discourse*

in the icy moment of desiring, a familiar
feeling thaws my veins. you:
except
it is no longer you i desire.

it is this body i have found,
that i am leaning on. a new

support system. just for this
        evening. how

must i keep you in moments like these,
when i search for your grainy moan in lips
that look similar but sound
                                        airy
like they could float away.

stupid lover
useless body
fatigued of language
i do nothing   but wait

and germinate
while seasons wrap themselves
around this year

so much, so much
has happened in the wasted
        moments
ants were quick to gather things
caterpillars curled into sheets
a mafia of wild monkeys scratched
the neighbour's dog
to death
lizards ravaged moths too foolish to run
                too incompetent to pick up the light and fly
apples have fallen and
bananas have moored to the shore

a whole new year
is skirting at the border
ready to pull up

Absent Person Stares at Her Antidepressants

Five oval circles sausaged together, linked
through metal and plastic strips. Serotonin
and happy hormones tucked into each
capsule, rolled tightly, resting peacefully.

Absent Person stares at them lecherously.
No shame, no manners.

Absent Person's mouth waters in anticipation.
Cannot wait to rip the seal apart, to place a pill
on her tongue (legitimately this time), cannot
wait for happiness to pilfer out, unravel, stretch across
saliva and flesh, cannot wait for JOY! POSITIVITY!
to sail through her bloodstream, cannot wait to be,
finally, a Person. In the Present. All here. Not escaping.
Cannot wait cannot wait cannot wait cannot wait.

Excitement bubbles wildly into a frothing monster hovering
over her head and now, Absent Person is fearful. She stares
at the plain green pills resting on a plain table in a plain room
compact with plain walls. All in her own home, all of it her own
choice, after all this education even—the prison resembles the
factory,
which resembles the school, which resembles the barracks,
which

resembles the hospital and so forth—all of this blankness
belongs
to her, all of it was made by her.

Absent Person stares at her antidepressants. Absence is a plain
cloud foaming,
seething above her. Presence is sorrowful, grey, but when burst
open, only
rains joy. Absent Person cannot wait for the monsoon season to
arrive.
Local authorities say it's around the corner. Summer should be
over soon.

Panic Attacks

The umbilical line shivers under water, divides
the sea to deliver the message. She receives it:
sweat falls down her neck in the dead of night.

It's morning for me. I'm scrubbing my face, the
water is boiling, the weather is cold, the heart
palpitating. At the beaches near us, the sea growls.

Self-Portrait
After A.K. Ramanujan

Shop windows recoil, the mirror trembles,
cracks, crumbles, leaves the body disgruntled.
(No, i don't know if i have gained weight or not,
if i've gotten darker or what kind of job i want,

what kind of poetry i write). This is the glamour
of being an absent person: all my temporary lives
jostle against each other, fighting for representation.
Thank god for this glorified I i'm trained to find—

thank god for this colonised mind. When able to,
i see myself in blackboards, pillow covers, writing
paper. Check my hair in cemented floors, floss in front
of plain brick walls, redo my makeup while sleeping.

The other day, i was underground and, in the opacity,
was startled to find that i'd never looked better.

Prime Minister, at Night, By Himself

stretches the short blanket
as much as possible—
the shroud doesn't fit his body

stacks up his days
like fresh styrofoam plates
one atop the other

plays with matchsticks
burns down hand-drawn maps
prays to his forgotten father

secures his hands in gloves
so he does not shock himself
with his own touch

who he really is
leaks out
wouldn't you love him now

இரண்டு
Fighting Absence, Finding Presence

No, I'm not going to
delve deep down and discover
I'm really de Souza Prabhu
even if Prabhu was no fool
and got the best of both worlds
(Catholic Brahmin!
I can hear his fat chuckle still.)

No matter that
my name is Greek
my surname Portuguese
my language alien.
There are ways
of belonging.

–from De *Souza Prabhu* by Eunice de Souza

ஜயமுண்டு பயமில்லை மனமே-இந்த
ஜன்மத்திலே விடுதலையுண்டு நிலையுண்டு.

பயனுண்டு பக்தியினாலே-நெஞ்சிற்
பதிவுற்றற குலசக்தி சரணுண்டு பகையில்லை.

–from ஜயமுண்டு பயமில்லை by சுப்பிரமணிய பாரதியார்

Outside the Prabhadevi Mandir

Outside the Prabhadevi mandir, everything
is saffron: Lakshmi's wicker basket of genda phool,
the *BAL THACKERAY VADA PAV STALL*,
Rafiul Islam's *Juice Stand* banner (also his orange juice),
and the controversial nagda putla standing proudly up
ahead, at the border of Cadell Road. Everything saffron
-ised, everything the same as it's always been, only
slightly modified. To keep up with the times. For instance,
the cows—Gowri, Sita, Komal, Radha—have been
grazing on the concrete street, half-asleep, for years.
But the saffron प्रभादेवी statue sign rose from the ground
some time between 2015 and 2019, years I spent studying
in Sonepat, searching for what it means to be at home,
what it means to have opinions, what it means to have
a nation. Everything the same as it's always been,
only now slightly modified. For instance, I still spend
my evenings outside the Prabhadevi mandir. Only
difference: I do not have tears to shed, I do not have
anything to ask for, I do not have any reason to hold
onto sadness. Around me, friends order mango milkshakes
and mosambi juices. Without sugar. Tejas gives me a hug,
and I see the devi smiling at me from inside.
Yesterday, Sakshi Mallik was dragged away mid-protest
while Modi dragged a saffron clan into the new Parliament.
Today at home, I lit the villakku at 6 p.m. sharp, and saw

Muruga's vel in its flame. Outside the Prabhadevi mandir, Rafiul Islam accepts my ₹200 note and offers me a genda phool in return. Devi ke liye, he says. An exchange done entirely in saffron. And my friends and I, we're still outside drinking mango milkshake and mosambi juice, making plans for this weekend. So I don't enter the temple just yet.

That is for me to do alone.

After the Riots

JAI HIND   BHARAT MATA KI JAI   JANA GANA
the streets   long sticks of chocolate
drizzled   with blood   sticky and sweet

kameezes   in pieces   covering
drains and pebbles   rid them of their sins
placards   bruised and aged   some

with sharper   ends   stuck in bodies
bursting through   bodies   half-open
half-closed   intestines   scribbled   splattered

on the streets   weakly echoing   anthems
uteruses   bloody   bitten   pulled out
of their homes   splayed out

for all to see burnt breasts hungry
toddlers crawl over charred teats
worry not it's time to clean up the streets

bring your badge your baton bring
your flag your language your song
we will clean up the mess worry not

bring them all out bring the saviours
bring the soldiers let us take back what is ours
we will rewrite the story the script

it's time to clean up the streets

The Etymology of a Word

IRE

a spinning sea

a flirtatious sea

a dirty-mouthed sea

SEDITION

bottled water

rationed water

denied water

I'm in an Uber at Two in the Morning and These Are Some Things My Cabbie Tells Me

'Let me tell you why I voted for Kamal. He promised us laptops. Toilets. Houses. UP could have been much richer than it is today, it could have been much richer than even Bombay. But dekho, Haath was full of corruption. See here, this Bandra–Worli sealink. Even now, at 2 a.m., there are so many cars, so many people out. Everyone here has roti-kapda-makaan. Now, in UP also, everyone will have. Yes, this Hindu-Muslim jhagda is bad, but I am not against Muslims. See, my taxi number ends with 6, my best friend's ends with 7. He is Muslim. We learnt driving together. We live together, with 5 other people. Here only, in Virar. So I am not against Muslims. If you ask me, I think that only Kamal will make UP rich. You know, now they are making a film city also there. Amitabh Bachchan, Shah Rukh Khan, Madhuri Dixit, will all come to UP. Just you see. Good things will happen, I know.'

Bombay Prayer, 2008
After Francisco X. Alarcón

something
was wrong
when we couldn't
see the sun

the sea
no longer
held up light
in her palms

night
went on
for three
days straight

how easy
hands
became
weapons

no moon
no howling dogs
only gunshots
tarring the sky

the whole city
an open wound
bleeding
never clotting

and us
20 million people
unmoving
with bated breath

how we stared
at each other
how we stared
and stared

Sunita Aunty

The sound of Marathi tumbling into my house,
a rough dialect from Raigarh cut and sharpened
by Bombay's glassy English, tells me Sunita Aunty
has arrived. Her mouth breaks apart when she sees
me. Limping across the hall, she hugs me and I feel
her back bent more than the last time I saw her, ever since
her roof collapsed. 'You know I carry the whole house,
what to do,' her voice squeezes through her throat,
hardened by years of pollution—this city's complimentary
dish. Sunita Aunty has brought homemade sheera
for dessert. 'I have added banana, but don't worry,
it's not too sweet like how those Brahmins make it.
They don't understand the delicious spice of flavour.
They put sugar in everything.' We eat sheera—that's not
too sweet—and talk current affairs, talk of Lakhimpur
Kheri and Hathras, and Sunita Aunty's eyes become opaque.
'It is terrible, what happens to Dalits, but you don't know
how it is in reality–how they get everything for free,
from college admissions to train seats to jobs.' Just then,
her Nokia ringtone slices our conversation in half.
She sighs a sigh that means it's the husband, picks up
and presses her knee, shakes her head, mutters quietly:
'Those gunda politicians came to our chawl again to beg
us to vote for them. Just like every year. Gunde-log. But
we are not fools. We know it's all bullshit. They are
casteless, spineless, heartless. They built us a building made

of cotton walls and cotton roofs that fly away or thin down in the rain and crumble over us.' Sunita Aunty is too angry now to eat sheera or talk about current affairs or share any recipes. Thunder flashes outside like a film camera. The rains are tiptoeing their way towards us now.

Parlour Aunty Told Me I Look Like a Man So I Stormed Out in Anger (Also Crying) and Here's What I Saw on My Way Home

A bouquet of men throng outside
Wimpy Wines. Longing arms wilt
outward to grab the closest bottle,

the darkest liquor, the most pungent
spirit. Blooming backwards, their bodies
bend at the stem, fall on the street,

shed colour onto the footpath. But their
eyes, they stick upward, black buds
reaching towards the gleaming yellow

bulb hanging over Wimpy Wines (the sun
never sets over Prabhadevi's favourite
theka). You can smell it before you see

it: this dishevelled cluster of flowers
(gulmohars and mallipoo and copper pods)
peppered over fallen copper wires,

frayed cables, and puddles of oil
and water pooling together far too closely.
The stench lingers in the air and travels

through crows' beaks. The birds gnaw
at anything that resembles flesh, flitter
from body to body until they hover

above my head. What am I doing here,
I wonder, in this slanted body, this
pieced-together frame of male and female,

seeking comfort at the end of my
lane. Just before it gets too dark, too drunk,
too full of despair. Just before autumn

comes storming in, peeling petals
from flowers, skin from bodies, gender
from flesh. Before I am noticed, I cower

away, trail on home. Appa is there, picking
பூ from the Swami Room, his hands
sparrowing from one moorthi to the next,

carefully plucking the red hibiscuses and
orange சாமந்திப்பூ and white மல்லிப்பூ
hidden between the gods, shared between

their outreached hands. He's made dinner,
he says. Eat properly, he says. It's a little salty
but overall okay, he says. When he looks

at me like this, like a bright mind energised
by ideas, forgetting it belongs to an ageing body,
I am reminded of myself. We share the same

face, appa and I, the same eyes, the same
droopy mouth. The same restless hands possess
us both, steering us away from consistency.

We're swept away by the frantic need to do, and do
now. Our love for languages—his, math,
mine, poetry—constantly jostles against

our maya-driven, caffeinated legs perpetually
running to grey offices and grey meetings.
Such is the fate of those of us who cannot wait,

who refuse to bloom when the conditions are
just right, who rebel against sunlight and water,
who sprout oddly, wrongly, in somersaulted bodies.

Nights at the Delhi Border

and when i sit here for hours
peering at this pavement puddle of water
i see in it a quiver a shiver a ripple of laughter
a sailing wrapper
a broken adaptor
an angrily torn piece from an angrily written love letter
a sinfully used piece of rubber
drops of semen courtesy of a nearby lecher
sweat dribbling down from the shoe-shining cobbler
wrinkled leaves that dived in (suicide's better
than surviving this summer)
spilt oil turning the puddle into a black mirror

i see in it those chilly nights of early december
and us waiting for what seemed like forever

at the unholy cusp of the city's border
for the shuttle to rescue us from turning into
FIVE YOUNG WOMEN'S BODIES FOUND OFF THE HIGHWAY AT AN UNGODLY HOUR

i see in it us waiting and looking down at the overflowing gutter
its pungent stench of vinyl chloride
thawing the air
growing stronger
reeking vapour
and strangling anything
that dares to wander near

the city is a dystopian disaster

and yet we find some reason to linger

to drift into laughter to pick apart
the stories of terror

to stand dangerously close
to the overflowing gutter

Summer in Horgen

In the place where nothing happens, nothing is happening
to us. Heatwaves scratched his body off this body

and I turned effervescent. I walked upside down,
underwater, I walked through continents.

This is a love poem.

This is an astonishment that however absent I am turned,
you remain. What bizarre seasons these have been, while
the monsoons have erased you into a watermark of who
you once were, my memories have dutifully coloured you in
every night. Every night, the train wheezes by every fifteen
minutes, vacuuming out this stationary apartment, silencing
the entire town, forcing prayer onto sceptics. Do they ever
feel cold in this glaring heat? Does summer also pierce their
skin? Do they all have a you to stop thinking about?

Here, an immense beauty surrounds me.
Here, all things are good and all things are fair.

This is the longest you haven't known where I am.
This is the longest you haven't known me.

Embers emanate from this volatile mind, distrusting its
own peeled body, soul standing bare before the lake.

I hope you see me.
I hope you see where I've been.

Fridays

i

on fridays, francisco is fed
up with san francisco—'fucking
prices just keep rising'—feeds
students either indian food
or mexican—'their flavours
are the best' he fervently
says—ensures that the kitchen
is forever a happy place
for all: bollywood music fizzles
through the grills, sizzling
heat onto every bacon patty:
a smell i am unused to, a place
i am new to. orders vapour around me.
outside it may be winter but in here
the stove stores summer, simmering
every half hour, time to restock,
time to work till francisco lets me leave
earlier than i should ('if you don't
tell elaine, it's all good'), if only he knew
i leave every time i mark myself
present on the ledger, every time the oven
opens and my skin is reminded
of home, i am turned absent, i am

ii

slipped out through boxed lunches,
i am losing
all memory that's recent, losing
place until i am in past
places, where friday afternoons
were us, at home, being
watched by the sea, seeing
neighbours while sipping
amma's coffee, amma, surveying
all three of our horoscopes, asking
why the year has only held pain, why
the planets aren't helping, hasn't
shani collected enough debt
from us, why he preys on those
who pray to him everyday—not
just saturdays. it's friday and she's
gone to him twice already, so

iii

maybe if i went
to shani he'll understand: both
of us born from darkness,
bastardised by our own bodies,
trying to perform
what we're here to do,
resisting erasure but wanting
it all the same, caught
between fight and fear,
tightroping light and shadow,
maybe if i go to shani
right now, this friday afternoon,
if i crawled out
through the termite-shaped hole
in the windowsill, he'll listen

to me, we'll talk over sunset,
he'll tell me about where
i might end up, maybe in a city
forced between hills and
forged out of poetry, a city
where i'll never be home,
never really tangible,

iv

where i am now, far
away from present places, amma,
appa, akka and i have nothing
much to say. san francisco feels
so far. home feels so slippery,
we sip our coffee, we look outside
the window, the beach is there,
like it is everyday. saturday is
tomorrow, like it is every week,
i am absent, like i am, all the time.

glossary

sanjana needed some space and
surya just wanted a pretty face.
so she created a clone
who took over while she wandered alone
thru the forests, years later
when she returned, the clone mothered
a son: shani. enraged, sanjana reduced
the clone to chaya, shadow of an obtuse
sun's glare, surya, discovering
whose shani really was, cursed him
into collecting human karma and debt:
making us pay for actions we repent.
but with a kind heart, sweet as honey,
no one's more misunderstood than shani.

Between the Last and First Local

i
The night we were out all night,
I kept thinking about
Dr Anant Joshi's diagnosis
stamped on my knees:
patellofemoral trochlear dysplasia,
and how good it felt, finally, to walk
my city from coastline to coastline,
thick night air licking my skin,
nursing my weathered femurs
and bundling us together.
Us: best friends, sisters, lovers,
brought to Bombay by migratory
winds, born during the monsoon
showers of 1997, born to a moody,
pendulum city, oscillating between
freshly cut land and a wrinkled sea.
To us, that night, Bombay was
our fiefdom. And to everyone else,
Bombay was theirs. It takes real
narcissists to find themselves
at the centre of a city so swollen
with people even at 2 a.m., 4 a.m., 5.47 a.m.,
a city folding out like a continent
that could only have been colonised
by the British: stupidly, mapped

and remapped, only to be eroded
of all monolithic power, fragmented
into mini kingdoms owned by
whoever happened to be standing
on that patch of land at that moment.
After nine hours of discovering
new cityscapes, a lighter sky trickled
through the air, seeping sobriety
into our bodies. My patellofemoral
knee pain was back and we were
at the edge of Bombay. Backs bent.
Eyes peering. Watching closely.

ii

The night we were out all night,
the dogs, the cops, the gods
competed in battle for territory,
put on a show, and presented their
best cases to us, the jury. Albeit
a little lost, a little unstable, we
were still a jury, nonetheless.
The gods sent yakshas to tell
us stories, sweet talk their way
into our thoughts. The dogs and
cops were tougher to adjudicate,
both resisting to explain themselves,
both far too superior for this sort
of showmanship. Both hungry,
both wandering with one eye open,
one ear close to the ground, always
alert, as though expecting something
devastating to happen at the sound
of every rising wave, every high tide.

iii

The night we were out all night,
we saw lovers at street corners.
Every kiss, every public display
of affection was an explosion
of love bursting, under film
banners and election posters.
One particular couple left
a trail of fireworks in Mahim,
at the intersection of the Sitladevi
mandir, Mahim dargah, and
St Michael's church. The very lane
where, 27 years ago, Appa—dark-
skinned man with a vague beard
and kada in hand—was stopped
in a kaali peeli by a mob. The men
were brandishing swords; silver
glistening in noon's sleepy sky.
Their screams setting off explosives,
burning gullies, bombing Bombay.
'Akka was one, Amma was home
with her. I had to make it back to Andheri
from Fort, but I didn't know if I would.
Should I tell them that my name is
Subramanian or Mohammad?' Appa's
story, every time it's told, leaves me
nameless. That night, when we were
out all night, the couple shared their
light with us. A young sun. A nebula
being birthed on the street. And I found
myself repeating 'I am Saranya. I am Saranya'.

A Story of Death

It's the heat, the goddamn biting heat, of this sick Tuesday afternoon, diseased with a rising temperature, that stabs Sivan more than */SARFAROSHI KI TAMANNA AB HUMAARE DIL MEIN HAI/* his mother's death has. Walking barefoot to the crematorium, tugging her body in the dead heat of summer, pinches his prickled feet. A lifetime ago they were gathered in black shoes that marched through white faces, */JAIHIND/* his hands carrying black flags, his words */SIMON GO BACK/* the black tar of sedition. In another life, Sivan was proudly taught */ KARO YA MARO/* to do or die. In this life he carries his mother on volcanic ground through a silent, staring city. Where are the chants, the fist-thumps now? Where */JAI JAWAN JAI KISAN/* are the young, the leaders now? Yet another woman, unlicensed, unregistered, is dragged through a city still mourning the riots of 2019 */ASHFAQUE AUR BISMIL KI YAARI/* or was it 2016 or 2002 or 1993 or 1975 or 1921 */INQUILAB ZINDABAD/* a city still reeling, still incurable. Sivan walks barefooted to the nearest crematorium */AARAM HARAM HAI/* still another kilometre away, suddenly chilly as his sweat falls over his mother's body. They could have left this wretched world together, gone where the lucky go, but

they */SAARE JAHAN SE ACCHA/* are here now. Falling at the crematorium's feet, Sivan surrenders both their lives. The official comes out. He wants proof. An ID, a license, a birth certificate */WRITE ME DOWN, I AM INDIAN/* anything will do. Sivan looks down at his empty palms and his mother's, their whole lives imprinted only within those ridges and grooves. What can he say about proof? That her fingers, burnt at the edges, prove that she was born some time during the forest fire of '54? How can he have proof /*HUM KAAGAZ NAHI DIKHAYENGE*/ when his mother, like him, is a tarnish on this landscape, when they live amongst forest jackals /*SWARAJ IS MY BIRTHRIGHT AND I SHALL HAVE IT*/ just as nameless, just as free. The official shows Sivan the door. Him and his mother are back in the desert of a city. Where /*HUM HONGE KAAMYAAB EK DIN*/ are all the people? The heat gets hotter, pouring drops of fire over his mother's body, setting

her alight, setting her free /*TUM MUJHE KHOON DO MAIN TUMHE AZAADI DOONGA*/. Ashes blanket the road in the shape of a body. Sivan carries it in his palms. A breeze caresses the city awake /*AT THE STROKE OF THE MIDNIGHT HOUR, INDIA WILL AWAKE TO LIFE AND FREEDOM*/ and the people come out. Licensed people, registered people. Important people. Lawyers, bankers, doctors, nurses, shop owners spill onto the streets. They watch Sivan slicing through the road. They /*HUM DEKHENGE*/ watch him walking back to the forest. They watch /*HUM DEKHENGE*/ him running into a field of jackals. They watch him /*HUM DEKHENGE*/ disappear. They carry on with their day.

What Do I Do With Yet Another Dead Moth In My Bathroom?

outside the window: a serpentine trail
of sunlight. soft flames river their way
towards our home. we are here,
absent people, visible at night.
i am here, an absent person, but i am
still here, sitting still. still waters
freeze in fear. outside, the hate speech
gets louder. hate, i learn, is not those
mobs that ash people down. it is
the casual shrug of the unaffected;
a single spark of apathy that, once lit,
can burn an entire forest down.

Prabhadevi Before Dawn

And to the everydayness of colour theory
and impressive histories of landscapes in
frames and framed landscapes, I raise
the stakes, I add another world. Here, water
is everywhere: in high tide rising at the
beach, dew peppering leaves, and buckets
filled with grumbling water, carried by
car cleaners through the streets.

At 5 a.m., Kunal and Savita Aunty unlock
the Amul dukaan. Rosy, the stray, blinks and waits
for Meena Aunty to bring her breakfast.
Celine, delivery woman and recovering addict,
is yelling first at her passed-out lover, then at
Raju dosawala to fuck her; it's the least he can
do if he can't pay her extra. Mohammad the watchman
tells her to shut up. Pathakji drags his fruit trolley
from the cornerstone chapel to under the holy banyan tree.
Sushma and Kishore slice fish at the koliwada,
set up shop at the bazaar before going off into the sea.
Raddhiwalas are up already: loading the factory
truck with recycled books and paper, getting their
kids ready for school. Pinky is smoking her first
cigarette of the day, right before switching on the
Siddhi Medical lights. A green cross shimmers silently.
Pappu Jain, Prabhadevi's sabzi wala, heads down

to the beach to brush his teeth while his good-for-nothing
son stumbles home with empty pockets. Thank god
for his daughter-in-law and thank god she speaks
english, he says, or else he'd have been a beggar.
Twelve-year-old Moin, angry at being awake this early,
stands before the makeshift maqbara for a minute, then
goes to buy milk for the entire family. Outside the temple,
Munna, the cow-herder, feeds Lakshmi and Gowri water,
quenching their thirst before their morning stroll begins.

Everything is black, so Monet must have been wrong: this is a portrait engorged with blackness. Black cats and bats mewl and howl, black roads roll out towards a pitch-black horizon, black goddesses and gods allow silence to thrive in a soon-to-be-gone, deep indigo sky.

Marathoners thunder through and the road
shudders in annoyance. Gulmohars fall off
tired trees, carpet the patchy, cracked
concrete yellow, and I'm convinced that
this is from where the sun must bloom.

மூன்று
Presence

நாத விந்துக லாதீ நமோநம
வேத மந்த்ரசொ ரூபா நமோநம
ஞான பண்டித ஸாமீ நமோநம
வெகுகோடி

– from *Thiruppugazh* by Arunaagirinathar

When He comes
Out of the blue
A meteorite
Shattering your home
Be sure
God is visiting you

–from *Says Tuka*, Tukaram, trans. Dilip Chitre

तूने मुझको बनाया
मैं तो जग को न भाया
तूने गले से लगाया
हक तू ही है खुदाया
सच तू ही है खुदाया

–from *Kun Faya Kun*, music by A.R. Rahman,
lyrics by Irshad Kamil

Navratri on the MUNI

Tired of rejecting your temporary home (denial is serious work), you
stretch your arms wide and embrace the fog, stop the 31, and accept
that you're eating a bagel and drinking a coffee. No milk. The blasphemy.

Yes, this is temporary, and yes, you shouldn't be here, and yes, you came
here just to leave, but you are here now, and it is Navratri, a new year,
and you are still here. And exhausted after rejecting yet another

temporary life, you turn the blue MUNI seats into a kovil of your own:
a kovil in transit—*things standing shall fall, but the moving ever shall stay*
—and realise that Basavanna was writing for you. Way before there were

buses and aeroplanes and nation states and passports and visas and
immigration, he was writing for you. His poetry stands for you. And
even though you are far from home, the distance is unable to take

your prayer away: the one you say every time you feel alone. Which
has happened in every city you have stepped into, every new identity
you have created—*my legs are pillars/the body the shrine/the head*

a cupola/of gold—every place of worship you've built in transit. Today,
bagel and coffee in hand, you mutter all 108 names from the Durga Ashtothram
inside this makeshift MUNI kovil, and suddenly you remember doing this

on the Mumbai local, the Delhi metro, the Bengaluru metro, the Sonepat
shuttle, the Chennai MTC, the Bombay BEST, the Zurich SBB, the London
tube, the Vancouver Translink. You remember the same restlessness,

the same frustration of not having reached, of waiting to get home, of never
really being at home for some fucking reason, and you sing out in sorrow
at how surreal this has been so far, you sing out in exasperation, you sing

out the same song every, every time—என்ன கவி பாடினாலும், உந்தன் மனம்
இரங்கவில்லை—you sing out, you sing to Muruga, Muruga, can you hear me,
can you hear me calling you, can you see me in this MUNI, can you bring me home?

After Kabir

listen:
it happened early—

sunrise tore through clouds,
bruised the sky, clotting it purple—

while they brandished paper,
while they sharpened songs,

while green and saffron flags competed
to paint Varanasi whole,

while crematoriums huffed and puffed,
while cemeteries pushed their nails into earth,

while petty men,
puzzled by bhakti,

pulled and clawed
at the stretcher,

that suddenly, the cloth
jumped off. revealing

a body
of flowers.

the sky, healing and paling,
gleamed.

the men, stunned.
their hands, turned

useless—laughable, even—
limping at their sides.

Varanasi, brought
to an apocalyptic

silence. Kabir, already
with his Ram.

ना तीरथ में ना मूरत में, ना एकांत निवास में ।
ना मंदिर में, ना मस्जिद में, ना काबे कैलाश में ॥

खोजी होए तुरत मिल जाऊं एक पल की ही तलाश में ।
कहे कबीर सुनो भाई साधो, मैं तो हूँ विश्वास में ॥
–कबीर दास

6 p.m.

a
diya/
one thick
wick/ a few
drops of oil/ one
matchbox/ a match
inside, and another one
to spare/ still air/ no open
windows and no hard breaths/
you smell the sweet stench first/
you see the small spark second/ that
blooms/ into a flame with wild petals
unravelling/ reaching out for more
evening sky/ licking the walls
of darkness dry

Early Morning Alarms

A vignette of kindness: you and Vanika are walking down
Prabhadevi's slippery, post-rain lanes, and your knee gives
way, yet again. Bending legs are a treacherous thing, and
the ground is harsh enough to make you lose faith. When
a bearded man, sleeping right there, startles at your cry,
offers you a Bisleri. After Indra has given the city unending
storms, it's rare to find mortals actually sharing water with
each other. You take a sip. Clouds clear out. You walk again.
San Francisco's moist fog corrodes everything—

concrete, tar, sand, chalk—until they are velvety
pastes of what they once were. Every morning,
the fog carries this scent to you, and your nose
jolts at the shock of memory. You're at the Adyar
house and know that it's light outside when
the moon comes down and settles on Amma's
hands holding kolam maavu; a watery moon,

a velvety moon, made from chalk-water paste,
drawn into intricate kolams outside every home.
Or how about right now, this immense presence

as an alarm—what better way to wake up to
today, than today. Today, the ducks are sitting
question marks circumferencing the pond,
asking when the sun will be out again, when it will
be time to swim again, when the tortoises will
be back again. You watch them and wonder how
much money it took to recreate nature in this
manicured garden. How much it takes to recreate
presence in this manicured body. What the cost
is, of finding peace. What to do once you have it.

ஜாதகம்

ONE?	AMMA	WON'T	YOU
INTO			MEET
DISSOLVE			ME
I	AND	YOU	WHERE

Layering Up in October

in this city of parks, it's always summer
when you least expect it. i never expect
to see the sun, so i'm always layered up
against something or the other: the cold, the tan,
the stares, the body. being seen.

in front of me, fifteen tiny turtles
huddle up on one big turtle. to my right,
long green leaves armour up around
a bush of scarlet flowers. below, a painted
road smoothens the tar; white lines

directing us where to go. but the sun
burns on today, vapourising
all coats and jackets. today, spreckels lake
is a shining mirror. in it: an elastic body
finally at one with water.

everything else peels away: the sun
-screen, the skin underneath,
the flesh and bones holding blood,
the voice screaming 'Well, Lacan Would Say …', the tired
brain wanting rest, the tired smile melting
off this face. everything is peeled off,
spiralling like pencil shavings into the lake.

i am a bare fruit ripening in this heat.
sunrays puncture through, clot this restless
mind into stillness, inject colour
into this monochromatic heart. a bruised stone
soaking in summer, turning yellow—

a bright mango seed, a hardened core
found on the ground, secreting aamras. resting
by the lake, uncovered, unlayered. a forgotten sun,
a forlorn sun. giving light, like it always does.

Autobiography
After Arun Kolatkar

my name is ___.
most days, i spend
far too much energy
screaming out my opinions.
most days, i don't even know
what my opinions
really are.

Instructions for Him for When He Reads These Poems and Finds that He's in Every One of Them

- Bend outwards, flail your body into a curve, become the sandy coastline that wages war with seawaves: the earth's first territorial battle.
- Bead these poems together into a rudraksh. Raise them to god and ask her what she thinks of them. They need critical feedback.
- Decide: either find your life in forms and documentation, or map it here, line by line, connect the dots, chart out your future and save the constellation you make.
- Quell the active, truth-telling voice in your head, sequester it into silence. Sometimes lying is the best thing you can do for me.
- Take a break from reading and go outside for a walk. Walk by the lake, walk around the park, walk everywhere you go walking at least ten times, walk yourself out, walk in circles, walk until you find some semblance of some horizon at some corner, and then walk into that.
- Lend a shoulder to a bumblebee some time. Carefully listen to what she has to say. Write all of it down, all the buzzing. Write like you might be stung. Write like the whole world is one nectar-filled sunflower.

- Rage into the wild. When that heats up your spinal column, all the way to your brain, allow it to melt, let the tears collect, breathe deeply. These are not easy poems to read. They anger me too.
- Walk backwards into kindergarten, settle down in the corner and listen to your teacher sharing knowledge on how to draw one house, one sun, three clouds, five birds, three mountains. Frame that picture. Fall back into it when this becomes too much.
- Remind yourself of every time you held me every time we almost ended, and hold these poems just like that.

Blue Gloves and Condensed Chicken Chettinad

It's been a long day, marked by pungence. Blue gloves
and condensed chicken chettinad have cling wrapped
themselves onto my sweaty palms. No matter how many
washes, some things stain, some smells remain. Everyone
around me exactly the same: Laura and Zulery exchange
makeup tips, Cheesa and Cheung on troublesome kids,
Justin and Chini grossed out by nuggets, Francisco and Jose
on call with the market, Elaine and Latasha prepping for
the audit. The cafeteria is silent to an absence. Clammy hands
and a heated oven remind me of a burning body. Such
a serious Monday, and I, such a cliche: horny at work,
dancing fingers twiddling on the table. The last time they did
that was on yet another man that wasn't you. These days,
I've been training this body to flatten outward, become
a stage. My hands dance all over, starting with just a touch
—a tiny raindrop rippling a puddle—on the tip of the third
toe of my left foot, the skeletal line behind my neck,
my breast, between my legs, over my clit, around my
arms. These days, I've been learning what an embrace is.
Since you're not here to teach me. Since I wrongly upheld you
as a teacher for so long. No matter how many years, the body
remembers. Some memories stain, some things remain.
Around me, Laura and Zulery and Cheesa and Cheung
and Justin and Chini and Francisco and Jose and Elaine and
Latasha all here, all present. Steaming pots of rice and dal,

an array of condiments, a hissing grill meditating behind
me, all here, all present. Blue gloves have clenched
these mundane monday palms. Hot chicken chettinad
exhales in exhaustion, fogs up the air, dews down my back,
fashions a wall between the cafeteria and myself. A tremor
sizzles down the spinal column. Desire washes the body.

Dadar Beach // Ocean Beach

the crab catchers catch crabs
by the sea, between the rocks,
with spindly legs, full of scabs,
collect them in an airtight box.

all the dogs are here, unleashed,
sand in their fur, stuck in their teeth.
and wild waves are labradors, running
towards us, excited: an ocean salivating.

at the fair, the stalls are colourful
lovers are by the shore, horses by the boats
& parents click snaps of gullible
kids, fighting at each others' throats.

a rare day of September sun
rains down hard on labour day
so moms and dads and daughters and sons
swim and tan before the sky caves away.

i run past mansions, piles of litter,
cows and joggers (whose pace beats mine),
imagine California's beaches, its weather,
and count down the days until i fly.

i run past mansions, abandoned joints,
joggers and surfers and bonfires crackling.
but i'm still cold; been far too spoilt
by Bombay's heat, perpetually raging.

Thatha Teaches Me Tamil

தமிழுக்கும்
His voice comes from the deep well
of his belly. Maybe that's where
he stores language. Maybe
that's where the prayer he sings
replenishes itself.

அமுதென்று
Muggy Chennai weather encloses us.
Dust hangs in the air. However
terrible the Madras summer gets,
the coffee only gets hotter.
A river of caffeine running down
my throat, a current of language
flowing the other way, moving up
to my tongue. I'm on holiday
and Thatha teaches me Tamil.

பேர்
The TV blares silently. It affects
Thatha and me too much: the news,
the politics, the vile. We both cry
too much. Bashir Badr's son died
of COVID. I wonder if his dementia
allows him to remember that. I wonder
if he cares that his Urdu shers and poems
are pawned by politicians in Parliament.

அந்த
Thatha despises Modi and distrusts
Mohammadens, but distrusts Modi
more. Thatha sings to his Pilayar, he
weeps to his devis. Thatha teaches
me to sing and weep. I learn
by process of imitation.

தமிழ்
Coffee, news and afternoon classes
go well with a plate of murukku.
Every piece looks like a Tamil letter.
ண, க, ல. I eat the letters, fried to perfection,
hoping it will help me learn faster.

இன்ப
Thatha tells me that when he was young, but old
enough to go to the cinema alone, his father
would tell him to watch only English movies. And study
only in English-medium schools. When the Brits left,
Thatha was 17 and Diwali crackled early into
the lanes of Madras. Everything was celebrated:
Pongal and Eid, Christmas and New Year's.

தமிழ்
When Murugan lost the race to Pilayar,
Thatha says, he was so jealous of his anna
that he ran away and hid in bhumilok,
on top of a hill. Until his parents found him,
he sang to the earthly people—
a new song in a whole new language.
Bursting from his mouth: a confetti
of words and alphabets, decorating
the land and sprinkling poetry on people.
Tamil was born that day.

எங்கள்
Thatha teaches me our history.
It is full of men.
I stop listening halfway.

உயிருக்கு
Thatha's patti would cook on fiery coal.

Thatha would ask her how she can withstand it.

She would say, 'பெண்களுடைய கை தான் நெருப்பு டா,'

—

female hands themselves are fire.

Poets live for their words and, in India, they die for them too.

நேர்
Thatha gulps the last of his coffee.
Ready to get up from his cane chair,
he calls out to Muruga.
He finds the strength to stand.

தமிழுக்கும் அமுதென்று பேர்-அந்தத் தமிழ்
இன்பத் தமிழ்எ ங்கள் உயிருக்கு நேர்.
-சுப்பிரமணிய பாரதியார்

‘பெண்களுடைய
கை தான்
நெருப்பு, டா’
-மீனாட்சி
பாட்டி

Elegy for When Nothing Else Can Be Done

Spent two years after graduation
walking in circles with Appa.
In a country so busy with disasters,
it's hard to keep up with the news;
every page is, after all, an obituary.
But we don't compare tragedies,
Appa and I, we just waste our time
tornadoing into yet another debate
on the latest communal attacks,
hospital fires, pandemic outbreaks,
or crying over the latest roster
of lost and found female bodies.

This is an endless, hourless, time
-less walk, and we walk around
the same building, walk around
the same family topics we always
avoid, walk in the rain and walk
in the anticipation of it. Pass Solkar,
head watchman, doing the books,
Pankaj, the maali prepping the
garden for monsoons, Meena,
Vyjayanthi, and Prajakta having
their bags checked at the gate,

the Rajagopals on their family
stroll, Billi, the cat, zipping around
on the prowl. Appa and I wave
to them with every round. Every
round an aarthi, a pradakshinam,
a ring on the same record I play on
repeat, every night in order to sleep.

Press the stylus in, turn up
the volume, the gramophone acting
as a loudspeaker during azaan.
So that everybody is invited.

An Inquiry into Tenderness

Lean into a cloud caressing your cheek.
Neatly fold sheets of sunlight and put them back

in your grandmother's cupboard. Wear them
as a sari on bizarre days. They will make

sense. Let go of the paper on your tongue.
Watch the enormous cake of words rise

in the oven of night. Sneak into the pool
of his voice. Who cares if it's past midnight.

It's yours. Everything is yours. Take a swim.
Vaseegara plays. You don't owe anyone

anything, you tell yourself, you keep telling
yourself. You're with your best friend on top

of a water tanker. Dusk is to come.
Who cares how you'll climb back down.

Notes

'Bombay Prayer' is inpsired by the poem 'L.A. Prayer' by Francisco X. Alarcón, in which he writes 'how easy/hands/ become/weapons'.

The Bharathiyar (சுப்பிரமணிய பாரதியார்) couplet that leads to 'Thatha Teaches Me Tamil' is from his song தமிழுக்கு அமுதென்று பேர் (*Thamizhukkum Amudhendru Per*), sung by P. Susheela for the 1956 film *Panchavarna Kili.*

'Overheard in Modi's India' is a golden shovel that uses the first line from Ilya Kaminsky's poem 'We Lived Happily During the War' from his collection *Deaf Republic*.

'Self-Portrait' is inspired by, and a direct referral to, 'Self-Portrait' by A.K. Ramanujan

'Night Windows' is an ekphrasis poem inspired by Edward Hopper's painting of the same name.

'Ghazal for the Absent Person – II' takes from both bhakti and sufi poetic traditions. The Tamil lines என்ன கவி பாடினாலும் உந்தன் மனம் இரங்கவில்லை. இன்னும் என்ன சோதனையா, முருகா! translate to: 'No matter how many poems I sing in praise of you, your heart doesn't melt and come down to me. How much more will you test my love, Muruga?' They come from a tamil bhakti song composed by Anayampatti Adisesha Iyer in Raga Neelami. The version that I am inspired by is sung by Madurai Somu.

In the last couplet, I quote the famous Hindi/Urdu idiom दिल्ली अभी दूर है/ हनूज़ दिली दुरस्त: 'Dilli abhi door hai' (Hindi). Originally 'Hanooz Dilli door ast' (Persian), a poem by Sufi saint Nizamuddin Auliya, circa 1320 CE, it means 'Delhi is still far away'. Auliya famously wrote it when Sultan Ghiyasuddin was returning to the capital after brutally winning a war. Funnily enough, the Sultan died on his way to Delhi. He never made it home.

'Navratri on the MUNI' references Vachana 820 by Basavanna, which has the famous saying "things standing shall fall, but the moving ever shall stay".

'After Kabir' is a poem I wrote because I've been enamoured with the folktale on what happened after Kabir's death in 1518. Apparently, both Hindu and Muslim groups were fighting over the mystic saint's body, since the former cremates and the latter buries their dead. However, upon uncovering the white cloth, all they found was a bed of flowers. I found the lines from Kabir Das's song, मोको कहां ढूँढे रे बन्दे (ना तीरथ में ना मूरत में, ना एकांत निवास में । ना मंदिर में, ना मस्जिद में, ना काबे कैलाश में ॥ खोजी होए तुरत मिल जाऊं एक पल की ही तलाश में । कहे कबीर सुनो भाई साधो, मैं तो हूँ विश्वास में ॥), to be most appropriate for this particular piece.

The epigraph in 'Stupid Lover', ('What thereby closes off the lover's language is the very thing which has instituted it: fascination') is taken from A Lover's Discourse by Roland Barthes, a literary philosophical book written in fragments, which explores the nature of love, the lover, and literature.

'My Name is Arun Kolatkar' is a poem by Arun Kolatkar that inspired me to write 'My Name is Saranya Subramanian'.

The poem 'ஜாதகம்' is written in the Tamil Vedic horoscopic structure. The first word of the poem, 'Amma', is placed where the moon resides in my personal horoscope. In Vedic astrology, the moon's position denotes one's relationship with their mother.

Acknowledgements

Thank you Anjum Hasan, my first poetry teacher, for all that you have taught me. Every time I write, your voice is in my head. Thank you DA Powell, Alan Chazaro, Derrick Austin and Lewis Buzbee: my incredible writing teachers who have been patient and generous with my work and have helped shape my voice. Thank you Preeti Vangani and Jennifer S. Cheng for seeing this collection in every shape and form, no matter how ugly or incomplete, and for helping me see it through to some form of finality. Thank you to my MFA cohort—Sarah, Neal, Leo, Calaghan, Bobbie, Sydney, Katie, Allison, TS—I am terrified of the writer I would have been without each of you. Thank you to the entire MFA writing community at the University of San Francisco that kept things afloat during the first two years of the pandemic when the entire world was drowning. Thank you to Professors Joost, Saikat, Rita, Madhavi, Abir, and the entire English department (faculty and students) at Ashoka University: the smartest people I will ever know, who taught me how to read and question. Thank you Tushna for helping me arrive at realisation, for teaching me how to un-seek absence. Thank you to my family, my thathas and pattis and mamus and mimmis and chittis and chittappas and athais and athimbers and cousins, who religiously read everything I write, without judgement. Thank you to friends who have grown me up: Sumee, Vanix, Zenia, Kaavya; friends who have made up my own coven of homes: Varsha, Vaishu, Noddy; and friends who have been personal editors over the years: Neha, Vasvi, Sheikh. Thank you Navaneeth for being part of this journey.

Thank you Radhika, Karthika and Jayapriya for believing in these poems and bringing this book to life. Thank you Adil, for the poetry and the conversations. Thank you Amma, Appa, Akka. I only write because of your unconditional, unprejudiced support. Thank you to everyone who has ever taken the time to read these little, inconsequential things I write. It is the biggest blessing to be read.

I am grateful to the following journals that have published some version of the following poems:

Aainanagar: 'Ghazal for the Absent Person – I' and 'Ghazal for the Absent Person – II'

Outlook Weekend: 'Prabhadevi Before Dawn' and 'Thatha Teaches Me Tamil'

Vayavya: 'Sunita Aunty'

Writing for Peace: 'After the Riots'

Gulmohur Quarterly: Parlour Aunty Told Me I Look Like a Man So I Stormed Out in Anger (Also Crying) and Here's What I Saw on My Way Home'

Madras Courier: 'Outside the Prabhadevi Mandir'

The Bombay Literary Magazine: 'Navratri on the Muni', 'Layering Up in October', 'Blue Gloves and Condensed Chicken Chettinad'.